improve
your verbal
reasoning

Jeremy Kourdi and Julie Kourdi

Hodder Education

338 Euston Road, London NW1 3BH.

Hodder Education is an Hachette UK company

First published in UK 2011 by Hodder Education.

This edition published 2011.

Copyright © 2011 Jeremy Kourdi and Julie Kourdi

British Library Cataloguing in Publication Data: a catalogue record for this title is available from the British Library.

10 9 8 7 6 5 4 3 2 1

www.hoddereducation.co.uk

Typeset by Cenveo Publisher Services.

Printed in Great Britain by CPI Cox & Wyman, Reading.

AYL

Contents

1

introduction

The key to succeeding with verbal reasoning and other types of test is surely honest self-reflection, openness and a desire to learn, develop and improve. By reading and working through this book you will be doing many of the things vital for success in this area, for example: building confidence, improving your mental agility, developing your skills at pattern recognition, enhancing your grammar and use of English, building your communication skills and understanding how to succeed with specific techniques and tests.

These skills are generally important for personal development and fulfilment as well as professional success, but they are specifically relevant for job interviews and assessment centres for career promotion. Verbal reasoning is not simply about communicating, vital though that is; it is also about the ability to think logically, critically, analytically – and successfully.

About verbal reasoning tests

Verbal reasoning tests are designed to measure a candidate's ability to use language and comprehend using the written word. At a simple level, this involves testing basic literacy, primarily the ability to write grammatically correct sentences, to spell and use punctuation correctly. However, at a more advanced level verbal reasoning tests are designed to assess a candidate's ability to understand the meaning of what has been written or said.

Employers are increasingly using verbal reasoning tests as part of their recruitment and assessment processes. Such tests are seen as providing a clear, objective assessment of a candidate's strengths and weaknesses, complementing other techniques such as interviews and psychometric personality tests. Verbal reasoning tests are particularly valued as they check comprehension and use of written English, providing an insight into a candidate's word power. Tests are a vital aspect of many jobs, whether in the public or private sector, large organizations or small. They are relevant for graduates seeking their first job as well as for employees looking for promotion. However, it is very easy to under-perform in verbal reasoning tests by being ill-prepared; what is not well known is that it is perfectly possible to improve your score with preparation and practice. This book will help you maximize your ability and the likelihood that you will succeed by:

* Enabling you to practise answering the various types of question that are set, within a fixed time limit.
* Helping you to analyse your current ability and improve performance.
* Showing how the different types of verbal reasoning test are set and marked, and how scores can be improved.
* Providing practical tips, techniques and explanations, as well as highlighting common pitfalls.

Knowing what to expect and being ready to work effectively through verbal reasoning tests is the key to success.

There are a few useful points to note about verbal reasoning tests:

* While many different versions of English are in everyday usage (including dialects, informal speech and specialist technical language or jargon), in verbal reasoning tests it is your ability to function effectively in 'standard English' which is being assessed.
* Tests are typically used together with other forms of assessment when making decisions about employment or promotion. While a good performance can help you to build a compelling case, it is worth remembering that a modest test performance can be offset by your previous work or life experience, your qualifications, performance at interview or suitability for the specific role.
* These tests are designed to help you prepare for verbal reasoning tests. They should enable you to learn how to cope with the time pressures you will experience in test conditions. For this reason, the instructions for each type of test include information about the amount of time that you should allow.
* These tests will help you improve your word power.
* They also include two logic tests that are designed to assess your skills of verbal reasoning. Understanding the different types of test you are likely to encounter and how you might improve are the primary purposes of these tests.

Preparing for the tests

So, what are the main principles that will ensure success at verbal reasoning? While there are many varied techniques and tips, several factors stand out as being consistently significant.

* *Be positive and confident.* The key is generally to remain calm, look for patterns and trends, and be willing to follow through a particular idea or thought.

* *Balance analysis and reasoning with intuition.* There may be times in the toughest tests when certainty eludes you, or when you find it difficult to 'get into' the test. Be willing to trust your sub-conscious, intuition or your first thought. It may be that you noticed something sub-consciously, or if not it does at least provide a starting point.

* *Question.* Are there patterns or relationships between words? Are there clues in the words? Why is this approach wrong?

* *Practice.* Practising will help improve your ability quite considerably; your mind will become better developed and stronger in this area. Practising will help tune your approach and thinking to the mindset of a psychometric tester, it will get you on the right wavelength and prepare you for the different types of test that you may encounter.

* *Develop your speed.* It may help to set clear goals when practising psychometric tests and among the most valuable goals is the ability to work faster and with greater accuracy. It is also worth pushing yourself, for example, by focusing on your timing as this is a critically important area with testing.

* *Look for opportunities to build your skills.* Psychometric tests in general and verbal reasoning tests in particular are specifically formulated, but you can improve your general abilities with a range of stretching mental activities. This fact holds the final key to succeeding at verbal reasoning tests: enjoy yourself.

2

timed tests

This section comprises a variety of tests designed both to enable you to practise your verbal reasoning skills as well as gaining an understanding of the different ways your skills can be tested. These tests will assess your comprehension and use of the English language, including grammatical understanding and stylistic awareness. You will be tested on your ability to recognize words and their opposites and distinguish between similar and competing information as well as your attention to detail and the ability to identify connections between different words. They will also test your understanding of complex information and critical reasoning, alongside the ability to manipulate data and use this to solve problems. It is important to read the instructions carefully and to ensure you understand what the tests involve and are asking for before you begin. Good luck!

Synonyms and antonyms

Although they are not always used to test advanced verbal reasoning, spellings, synonyms and antonyms are valued as they provide a valuable guide to literacy levels. They also introduce the candidate to tests that can later become tougher, and provide a useful start for candidates who are new to advanced tests.

Synonyms

Tests 1-3 comprise synonym tests, each of 10 questions. In this type of test, the task is to identify the word with a similar meaning from the options provided. Each test should take no longer than three minutes.

Test 1

(Answers to this test can be found in Chapter 3)

1   Bellicose means the same as:
    a unwell b large c poisonous d aggressive

2   Blandishments means the same as:
    a errors b blasphemous c clarity d coaxing

3   Confabulate means the same as:
    a chat b make up c cheat d celebrate

4   Corrigible means the same as:
    a difficult b constructed c correctable d persuasive

5   Distil means the same as:
    a weaken b strengthen c purify d mix

6   Acrid means the same as:
    a dry b sharp c humid d dangerous

7   Aegis means the same as:
    a protection b traditional c pathos d final

8   Entrust means the same as:
    a agreement b contract c take from d delegate

9   Equivocate means the same as:
    a attempt b argue c evade d score

10 Deign means the same as:
    a disagree b consent c deride d honour

Test 2

(Answers to this test can be found in Chapter 3)

1. Improvise means the same as:
   a concoct b conduct c progress d deplete
2. Locus means the same as:
   a movement b expression c temporary d position
3. Disjointed means the same as:
   a removed b unconnected c released d discharged
4. Marked means the same as:
   a stung b saleable c notable d offered
5. Rein means the same as:
   a hegemony b restrain c precipitation
   d dominion
6. Submit means the same as:
   a assert b find c depart d remove
7. Protagonist means the same as:
   a competitor b enemy c worker d principal
8. Impugn means the same as:
   a obsolete b impale c impure d attack
9. Test means the same as:
   a correct b evaluate c match d effort
10. Amuse means the same as:
    a charm b entertain c hilarity d happy

Test 3

(Answers to this test can be found in Chapter 3)

1. Amenity is the same as:
   a ungenerous b without grace c amnesty
   d pleasantness
2. Slight is the same as:
   a trick b snub c bright d consider
3. Tide is the same as:
   a trend b wave c side d knotted
4. Trivia is the same as:
   a aspects b complexities c simplistic
   d minutiae

5   Upset is the same as:
    a feel b lose c agitate d revolve
6   Value is the same as:
    a regard b charge c expensive d worth
7   Vision is the same as:
    a eyes b dream c conduct d cutting
8   Spend is the same as:
    a hypothesize b disburse c guess d wager
9   Give is the same as:
    a surrender b evolve c examine d receive
10 Funny is the same as:
    a unlikely b tickle c odd d paltry

Antonyms

Tests 4-6 are **antonym** tests each of 10 sentences. In this type of test, the task is to identify the word with the opposite meaning from the options provided. Each test should take no longer than three minutes.

Test 4

(Answers to this test can be found in Chapter 3)

1   Anxious is the opposite of:
    a intent b watchful c careless d untoward
2   Treat is the opposite of:
    a ignore b celebrate c usage d trend
3   Pungent is the opposite of:
    a acute b poignant c sweet d concoction
4   Stalwart is the opposite of:
    a staunch b barrier c resolute d cowardly
5   Staid is the opposite of:
    a excitable b restrictive c fallow d unimportant
6   Require is the opposite of:
    a unfailing b bid c unnecessary d unreserved
7   Tacit is the opposite of:
    a implied b blank c undeclared d spoken

8 Strong is the opposite of:
a failed **b** disagreeable **c** tough **d** weak

9 Grate is the opposite of:
a shredded **b** grind **c** not annoying **d** unsatisfied

10 Drilled is the opposite of:
a emptied **b** untrained **c** rotated **d** unplugged

Test 5
(Answers to this test can be found in Chapter 3)

1 Flower is the opposite of:
a bloom **b** unappealing **c** undeveloped **d** unclear

2 Quietly is the opposite of:
a overtly **b** unsure **c** noiselessly **d** unobtrusive

3 Crowd is the opposite of:
a dislocation **b** dispel **c** distraction **d** distaff

4 Cheerful is the opposite of:
a blithe **b** animated **c** pessimistic **d** cold

5 Diffuse is the opposite of:
a abandoned **b** gathered **c** unabated **d** digressive

6 Satiated is the opposite of:
a derisive **b** resolute **c** caricature **d** unfulfilled

7 Fissured is the opposite of:
a intact **b** fiscal **c** held up **d** broken

8 Endanger is the opposite of:
a excess **b** hamper **c** imperil **d** secure

9 Creeping is the opposite of:
a fawning **b** suddenly **c** repulsed **d** instrumental

10 Project is the opposite of:
a withdraw **b** predict **c** bulge **d** estimate

Test 6
(Answers to this test can be found in Chapter 3)

1 Jilt is the opposite of:
a straight **b** soften **c** open **d** remain

2 Merge is the opposite of:
a absorption **b** meet **c** separate **d** leave

3 Oppose is the opposite of:
   a argue **b** agree **c** ascend **d** askew

4 Asinine is the opposite of:
   a sensible **b** fatuous **c** senseless **d** inane

5 Ascent is the opposite of:
   a graduating **b** climb **c** descent **d** domineering

6 Jejune is the opposite of:
   a sophisticated **b** early **c** boring **d** intrepid

7 Merciful is the opposite of:
   a unsettled **b** heavy **c** uncharitable **d** forbidding

8 Discriminating is the opposite of:
   a favoured **b** tasteful **c** inequity **d** insensitive

9 Persist is the opposite of:
   a insist **b** leave **c** resolve **d** purposeful

10 Roused is the opposite of:
   a unconscious **b** unfulfilled **c** provoked **d** staid

Word placement tests

Introduction

Word placement tests assess several skills, including:
spelling, grammar, punctuation and general English usage.
They require knowledge and an ability to distinguish between
similar and competing information. Tests 7-9 comprise three
tests each of 10 sentences. In each question, you need to put
the correct word in the right place. Allow yourself 5 minutes to
complete each test.

Test 7

(Answers to this test can be found in Chapter 3)

1 Place the words *they're* and/or *their*:

   I enjoy working with these people, _____
   professionalism is impressive and _____
   always interesting.

2 Place the words *discrete* and/or *discreet*:
   I will need to be _____ when compiling such _____ statistics.

3 Place the words *whose* and/or *who's*:
   _____ clothes are these, and _____ at the door?

4 Place the words *fair* and/or *fare*:
   It was a _____ day, and I had the correct change for my _____ on the bus.

5 Place the words *sail* and/or *sale*:
   The boat was on _____ because it needed a new _____.

6 Place the words *bail* and/or *bale*:
   Seth always had to _____ out Jamie when the _____ was too heavy for Jamie to lift.

7 Place the words *pried* and/or *pride*:
   The hunters always _____ into my affairs during my study into the _____ of lions that lived close to our research station.

8 Place the words *council* and/or *counsel*:
   Rosemary took legal _____ when she took her local _____ to court over refuse collection.

9 Place the word *counsellor* or *councillor*:
   After struggling with depression and psychological problems, Philip took his doctor's advice and visited a professional _____.

10 Place the word *incite* or *insight*:
    They showed remarkable _____ when developing their theory.

Test 8

(Answers to this test can be found in Chapter 3)

1 Place the words *alluded* and/or *eluded*:
   The meaning of the poem _____ the students, although the teacher had _____ to its meaning during the lesson.

2 Place the words *either* and/or *neither*:

When assessing performance, it is important to be _____ rude nor hostile. Otherwise, the result could be _____ demotivation or depression.

3 Place the word *stripped* or *striped*:

The birds _____ the tree of all its fruit.

4 Place the words *faint* and/or *feint*:

There was a _____ smell of gas in the air that made me feel queasy and _____.

5 Place the words *staring* and/or *starring*:

He found himself _____ at the woman who was _____ in the movie.

6 Place the words *vicious*, *viscose* or *viscous*:

It was hard work wading through the swamp, as the water felt _____.

7 Place the words *villein* and/or *villain*:

It was his personality that made him a _____, not the fact that he was a _____.

8 Place the word *vilify* or *vivify*:

A good animator will _____ a cartoon character, bringing it to life for the audience.

9 Place the words *vortex* and/or *vertex*:

The boat was stuck in a whirling _____, which could be seen from the advantage of the _____ above the cliff.

10 Place the word *veracity* or *voracity*:

Sam's _____ was greatly appreciated by the magistrate: it was just what the situation needed.

Test 9

(Answers to this test can be found in Chapter 3)

1 Place the words *dissent* and/or *descent*:

There was a great deal of _____ in the group about how to make the _____ down the mountain.

2   Place the words *ascent* and/or *assent*:
    I will need the team leader's _____ if I am
    to join the others making the _____ in the
    morning.

3   Place the word *ordinance* or *ordnance*:
    The new leader issued his first _____.

4   Place the word *elicit* or *illicit*:
    The police tried to _____ information from
    the suspects about their suspicious behaviour.

5   Place the word *compliment* or *complement*:
    Knowing whether one colour will _____
    another is important in fashion design.

6   Place the word *foundered* or *floundered*:
    The plan _____ at the last minute.

7   Place the word *weary* or *wary*:
    The long hours made everyone _____ that
    mistakes could be made.

8   Place the word *forward* or *foreword*:
    The start of the book encouraged people to
    move _____ with their career plans.

9   Place the words *affect* and/or *effect*:
    The long hours did _____ the staff, leading to
    the _____ of low morale and high turnover of
    staff.

10 Place the word *eminent* or *imminent*:
    Success was _____. It would not be long
    before the news would be announced.

Word swap tests

Introduction

Word swap tests are difficult, as they demand attention
to detail. They measure an ability to focus, to avoid distractions
and to remove irrelevant information. Tests 10–12 each contain
15 sentences. In each question, the position of two words has

been swapped so that the sentences no longer make sense. You have to read each sentence carefully, pick out the two words and underline them. Allow yourself 10 minutes to complete each test. When you have finished (or the time is up) check your score against the answers later in the book. At the end of each test, work through any questions that you answered incorrectly or you failed to complete in the time allowed.

Test 10

(Answers to this test can be found in Chapter 3)

1. As the airline became the established successor to the railway as a scope of transport, so the means of its commercial use increased.

2. In search of Americans money and career advancement, both are working harder than ever.

3. In ability to be a good pilot, a person must have developed the order to plan well ahead.

4. Remember, as we carry on pumping billions of tonnes of heat-trapping gases into the nature each year, how awesome the power of atmosphere can be.

5. We shall have cold salad at eight o'clock; there will be cold meat, cheese, supper and fruit.

6. There will always be the dark and tangled process in the decision-making stretches – mysterious even to those who may be intimately involved.

7. Strategic decisions are rarely straightforward or simple, because they involve people's judgements that depend to a large degree on value attitudes, perceptions and assumptions.

8. The firm argued in court that the computer held private information that should not fall into sensitive hands.

9. In many situations, however, the written amount and complexity of information require that it be transmitted in large form.

10 The group formed to plan the transport Christmas party was asked to investigate suitable venues, office and refreshments.

11 Electricity levels in London dropped last month, thanks to reduced road traffic and the shutting down of two pollution generating plants.

12 Tourists from the United States of America are frequently surprised by the public they perceive in security places in Britain.

13 The first standard that faced the explorers was to develop a test method to traverse crevasses.

14 The points deserve full credit for providing a clear, accurate summary of the main managers.

15 Amid eleventh-hour fears that war would break out, growing peace talks were held at the United Nations last night.

Test 11

(Answers to this test can be found in Chapter 3)

1 A polite sender not to open any e-mails or attachments where you do not recognize the reminder.

2 Not even snazzy changes of personnel seem able to dim the panache of this constant musical revival.

3 The movie director has played fast and loose with this particular surprise – it will amaze, genre and not fail to please.

4 Other ways of mitigating risks are to share them with a monitor, partner each risk or make contingency plans in case the risk becomes reality.

5 Once the inherent risks in a control have been understood, the priority is to exercise decision.

6 Significant skills in the numbers of people in both the developed and developing world will affect the size and dynamics of markets, and the value of many key reductions.

7   When there is a decreasing number of working people to fund jobs, retirement ages may need to change, and immigration may need to be encouraged to ensure that there are people to do the pensions that need to be done.

8   Recent years have seen a rise in the involvement of the Chief Finance Officer (CFO), to the point where virtually no major decision is made without the CFO's significance.

9   People and organizations now recognize that paradoxes can be technological, and they are more enabled to reconcile them than ever before, partly because of reconciled progress.

10   A vision must have the ability to create and communicate a convincing and realistic leader that will sustain an organization and its people through both good times and bad.

11   The conquests of the Mongol impact can hardly be over-estimated, although the swift arc of their ascendancy spanned only a hundred years.

12   Throughout its long history, the Roman state had to face continual military peoples from the warlike challenges on its frontiers.

13   As the Cold War dragged on and on, with a kind of ideological permafrost reassuringly over much of the world, many people on both sides of the divide came to view the situation as settling normal.

14   Because of its potential importance for navigation, the accurate business of obtaining whole star positions was of key importance in the late seventeenth century, both commercially and because of its military applications.

15 The team struggled day and night with her
researcher to find a statistically valid link that
would solve the problem and prove their theory.

Test 12
(Answers to this test can be found in Chapter 3)

1 Matter is certainly a topic that gets people
energized no trust where in the world they are, yet
despite this, it is rarely the subject of conversation
inside organizations.

2 Climate is changing in fundamental and
dangerous ways that may affect the planet of
power on the balance.

3 Business scenarios and economists predict a range
of varying pundits for the future of the work
environment, but there is one thing that all are
sure about: the future will be uncertain.

4 Albert Einstein once said that the most important
building that human beings can ask themselves
is whether the world is a friendly place or an
unfriendly place, for their answer to that question
determines whether they live their life question
bridges or building walls.

5 Corporate values are a genuine competitive
advantage, an enduring service amid so many
changes in product and factor.

6 With no individual, preordained career ladder for
the rigid to follow, the prospects of success cannot
be assumed.

7 As the Wall Street manager said to a young,
terrified trader who had just lost a million on the
trading room floor: 'Fire you? I just invested ten
fortune dollars in your future with this firm.'

8 Recent research has focused on promising the
biological mechanisms that underpin trusting

behaviour, and one finding approach has been to correlate variations in trust with changes in levels of eight hormones.

9   Stalin's rule, reinforced by a cult of apparatus, fought real and alleged opponents mainly through the security personality, such as the NKVD.

10 The hormone acts in parts of the system (such as the limbic brain and the pre-frontal cortex) associated with the emotions, memory and decision-making – all are essential for social interactions.

11 Global pandemics have always been with scale, the difference now is the speed and us of transmission and its resulting consequences, which could be unprecedented.

12 Unless you can influence senior people there is a degree that your job will never be more than reactive; to some meaningful danger you need to be in the driving seat of the relationship.

13 Manager's should never be forgotten therefore that it is as much in your it interest as it is in yours for you to work effectively together.

14 The US view of Europe's growth is broadly accurate: EU influence depends on economic future, managing immigration, and developing the German economy.

15 The Tudors valued crisis, and this mass urban migration represented a serious stability.

Missing word tests

Introduction

Missing word tests require a good knowledge of English, with questions relying on an understanding of several key areas – from spellings and definitions to tenses and punctuation. They demand attention to detail and an ability both to identify misleading information and to combine correct answers. Tests 13 and 14 each comprise 15 sentences. In this type of test, two gaps have been left in each sentence. Allow yourself 8 minutes to complete each test.

Test 13

(Answers to this test can be found in Chapter 3)

1. _____ a break from studies is important _____ ensure learning is effective and successful.

A	B	C	D	E
Take	Taking	Taken	Taking	none of the
so	for	for	to	above

2. The only measure of success is _____; the only means to _____ is success.

A	B	C	D	E
profit	profitable	profitability	profit	none
profitable	profit	profitability	profited	of the above

3. Athletics is a very demanding sport, _____ _____ discipline and determination.

A	B	C	D	E
requiring	require	requiring	require	none
immense	immense	immensely	immensely	of the above

4. The journalist knew that the events that _____ yesterday _____ decisive.

A	B	C	D	E
occur	unfolded	unfolded	occurred	none of
were	was	were	was	the above

5. The training course _____ give me the skills and confidence that will _____ me to put my views across in the meeting next week.

A	B	C	D	E
can't	will	never	will	none of
allowed	enable	allow	enabled	the above

6 The growth of the leisure industry _____ how important the _____ sector is to the modern economy; however, it relies on other parts of the economy performing well, too.

A	B	C
demonstrates	demonstrated	demonstrated
tertiary	sector	studying

D	E
demonstrates	none
tersiary	of the above

7 The recipe requires _____ coconut, which Peter_____ buying for me at the supermarket now.

A	B	C	D	E
dessicrated	desiccated	dessicated	dessicated	none
was	is	was	is	of the above

8 The fossil was found in one particular _____ of the rock, which was difficult for the geologist to _____.

A	B	C	D	E
stratum	strata	stratum	strata	none
excavate	excavate	excoriate	excoriate	of the above

9 I have _____ the report for you, I _____ it during my lunch break.

A	B	C	D	E
prepared	wrote	prepared	read	none of the
done	done	did	done	above

10 When I _____ the team, I found that to _____ is all about gaining trust.

A	B	C	D	E
lead	led	lead	led	none of the
lead	lead	led	led	above

11 The judges were given a few _____ for assessment, but the principal _____ was the decisive factor.

A	B	C	D	E
criteria	criteria	criteria	criterion	none of the
criteria	criterion	criterium	criteria	above

12 There were _____ vines, which meant _____ wine this year.

A	B	C	D	E
less	fewer	less	fewer	none of the
fewer	fewer	less	less	above

13 You _____ your lunch very quickly. I have _____ mine also.

A	B	C	D	E
eat	eaten	ate	eaten	none of the
ate	eaten	ate	ate	above

14 The problem seemed _____, due to the _____ nature of their differences.

A	B	C	D	E
intractable	intractible	intractable	intractible	none
irrevocible	irrevocible	irrevocable	irrevocable	of the
				above

15 The guard thought it was _____, as the _____ camera was still working.

A	B	C
all right	alright	alright
surveillance	surveyllance	surveilance

D	E
all right	none
surveilance	of the above

Test 14

(Answers to this test can be found in Chapter 3)

1 Sam_____ Marcy a book, whereas Sam was _____cologne from Amy.

A	B	C	D	E
given	gave	given	given	none of the
gave	gave	given	giving	above

2 To overcome the problem of outdated ammunition, the army needs better _____ if the battle _____ to be successful.

A	B	C	D	E
ordinance	ordnance	ordnance	ordinance	none
was	is	was	is	of the above

3 The _____ weather forecast predicts a _____ to reach shore at midnight.

A	B	C	D	E
current	currant	currant	current	none
destructive	hurricane	gale	hurricane	of the above

4 The movie _____ my favourite actor, so I _____ it.

A	B	C	D	E
stared	starred	stared	starred	none of
taped	taped	tapped	tapped	the above

5 _____ rosemary nor thyme would prosper in such wet soil. They both prefer more _____ conditions.

A	B	C	D	E
Neither	Either	Neither	Either	none of the
arrid	arid	arid	arrid	above

6 It is customary to use _____ for_____.

A	B	C
stationery	stationary	stationery
corespondence	correspondence	correspondance

D	E
stationary	none
correspondance	of the above

7 Despite his greed, his _____ in professional matters was admired, as truthfulness and reliability _____ important attributes.

A	B	C	D	E
voracity	veracity	voracity	veracity	none of the
was	were	were	was	above

8 The explorer was eager to find the _____ of the river; however, the _____ equipment hindered his efforts.

A	B	C	D	E
source	sauce	source	sauce	none of the
course	coarse	coarse	course	above

9 Paper-making relies on a sustainable policy regarding _____. _____ new techniques will ease this problem.

A	B	C	D	E
forests	environment	forrests	forrests	none
Maybe	Definitely	Maybe	Probable	of the above

10 The mathematics department was large, and the many _____ efforts were applied to equations solving problems in one _____.

A	B
mathematicians'	mathematician's
plain	plane

C	D	E
mathematicians'	mathematician's	none of the
plane	plain	above

11 The toxin administered was _____ and was noted for _____ therapeutic properties.

A	B	C	D	E
beneficial	non-lethal	beneficial	nonlethal	none
it's	treatment	its	it's	of the above

12 Her _____ was apparent in her indifferent _____. Clearly, her interests lay elsewhere.

A	B	C
nonchalence	nonchalance	nonchalance
manor	manor	manner

D	E
nonchalance	none of the
manner	above

13 The panel faced an _____ matter, full of _____ facts.

A
imponderable
contradictory

B
imponderible
contradictory

C
imponderable
contradictary

D
imponderable
contratdictary

E
none of the
above

14 _____ lessons are important for actors when they _____ to use a different accent.

A
Elocution
need

B
Election
need

C
Elocution
needed

D
Election
needed

E
none
of the
above

15 _____ is always nice to _____ from a friend.

A
Corespondance
recieve

B
Correspondance
receive

C
Correspondence
recieve

D
Correspondence
receive

E
none of the
above

Word relationship tests

Introduction

Word relationship tests assess the ability to identify a connection and then apply that connection to another set of words. These tests are often designed to mislead, so care must be taken. Tests 15-18 comprise four tests, each of 10 questions. In this type of test, the task is to identify the word that most closely forms a verbal analogy. In essence, a verbal analogy is an agreement, similarity or link between the meaning of words. Allow yourself 5 minutes to complete each test.

Test 15

(Answers to this test can be found in Chapter 3)

1 Paper is to tree as glass is to:
  a transparent **b** holder **c** sand **d** rim

2 Pen is to nib as telescope is to:
  a magnify **b** lens **c** image **d** space

3 File is to shape as brush is to:
  a cut **b** hair **c** dog **d** paint

4 Time is to second as volume is to:
  a millilitre **b** millisecond **c** noise **d** control

5 Storm is to calm as cloudy is to:
  a thunder **b** windy **c** teacup **d** clear

6 Current is to amp as temperature is to:
  a hot **b** Celsius **c** thermometer **d** heating

7 Soap is to fat as wine is to:
  a red **b** ferment **c** bottle **d** grape

8 Run is to track as swim is to:
  a pool **b** costume **c** stroke **d** chlorine

9 Fahrenheit is to centigrade as mile is to:
  a kelvin **b** distance **c** kilometre **d** length

10 Foot is to walk as scissors is to:
  a contract **b** divide **c** glue **d** knife

Test 16

(Answers to this test can be found in Chapter 3)

1 High temperature is to heat as sand is to:
  a glass **b** sandcastle **c** sand dune **d** erosion

2 Shampoo is to bottle as tea is to:
  a kettle **b** bag **c** leaf **d** golf ball

3 Foot is to shoe as house is to:
  a roof **b** home **c** accommodate **d** flat

4 Handle is to door as sunlight is to:
  a tan **b** moonlight **c** flare **d** spectrum

5 Fox is to cub as plant is to:
  a stalk **b** seedling **c** bush **d** flower

6 Road is to train as sky is to:
 a aeroplane **b** balloon **c** air **d** boat

7 Daffodil is to oak tree as village is to:
 a house **b** rural **c** church **d** city

8 Cane is to sugar as cabbage white is to:
 a potato **b** carrot **c** butterfly **d** root

9 Timid is to bold as dense is to:
 a stupidity **b** weight **c** height **d** diffuse

10 Tooth is to brush as air is to:
 a plane **b** jet engine **c** cloud **d** tree

In the next two tests, the format has been altered slightly, although the task remains to identify the word that most closely forms a verbal analogy (these are also known as 'word links tests'). Your task is to identify two words in the lower line, one in each half, which form a verbal analogy when paired with words in the upper line.

Test 17

(Answers to this test can be found in Chapter 3)

1 Ink Silk
 squid blue indelible material sheep worm

2 Money Petrol
 cash trade banker oil tank travel

3 Bull Person
 beef prairie herd mother people horse

4 Stable Shrewd
 horse steady instability stupid perceptive cute

5 Sea Emperor
 gull wet tide empire penguin king

6 Essay Dinner
 work teacher write breakfast recipe cook

7 Nature Nurture
 innate country wildlife genetics produced natural

8 Armoury Apple
 pistol soldier weapons stalk seeds skin

9 Cry Whisper
   baby laughed war bellowed breeze ear
10 Glass Concrete
   transparent glazier silica rigid pavement certain

Test 18

(Answers to this test can be found in Chapter 3)

1 Telephone Car
   bill video communicate Mercedes drive petrol
2 Bed Sofa
   snore sheets sleep cushions comfort large
3 Lava Ice
   seismological hot volcano glacier martini earth
4 Singer Lecturer
   instrument loud concert lecture group examination
5 Legislature Zoo
   parliamentarians laws ethics wild urban animals
6 Project Film
   budget manager throw story director cinema
7 Computer Airplane
   box spreadsheet software avionics airport passengers
8 Decision Problem
   thought crisis making solving help people
9 Snow Plants
   precipitation white chilly vegetation branch wood
10 Thorax Chest
   chemical insect operation pirate appendage primate

Logic tests

Introduction

Logic tests assess ability to understand complex issues, manipulate data and solve problems. Specifically, they measure precision in handling definitive detail and ability to draw conclusions from the evidence. Tests 19 and 20 comprise two tests each of 10 questions. In each question, the task is to use the information provided to logically deduce the correct answer. This is the most diverse selection of tests, including different styles of tests for critical reasoning, comprehension and problem-solving. Don't be distracted by the different types of test, simply work through them quickly and methodically, deducing the correct answer. When you have finished, check your score against the answers later in the book. At the end of each test, work through any questions that you answered incorrectly or you failed to complete in the time allowed. Allow yourself 20 minutes to complete each test.

Test 19

(Answers to this test can be found in Chapter 3)

1. David and Pat earn more money than Louise. Matt earns less than Louise. Derek earns more than Louise. Who earns the least money?
   a David b Pat c Louise d Matt e Derek

2. At an international conference, 1/5 of the people attending came from Africa. If the number of Europeans at the conference was 2/3 greater than the number of Africans, what fraction of people at the dinner were neither from Africa nor from Europe?
   a 1/5 b 2/5 c 7/15 d 8/15 e 2/3

3. Thomas is now 12 years younger than Julie. If in 9 years Julie will be twice as old as Thomas, how old will Thomas be in 4 years?
   a 3 b 7 c 15 d 21 e 25

4. The value of an antique picture increased by 30 per cent from 1999 to 2003 and then decreased by 20 per cent from 2003 to 2007. The picture's value in 2007 was what percentage of its value in 1999?
   a 90% b 100% c 104% d 110% e 124%

5. If the price of a car increased by 20 per cent, and then by a further 20 per cent, what percentage of the original price is the increase in price?
   a 24% b 30% c 40% d 44% e 67%

6 An insurance company provides coverage for a certain cosmetic procedure according to the following rules: the policy pays 80 per cent of the first $1,200 of cost, and 50 per cent of the cost above $1,200. If a patient had to pay $490 of the cost for this procedure herself, how much did the procedure cost?

   a $1,100 **b** $1,200 **c** $1,450 **d** $1,600 **e** $1,700

7 Working together, Rashid, Ahmed and Michael require $4^{1}/_{2}$ hours to finish a task, if each of them works at his respective constant rate. If Rashid alone can complete the task in 9 hours, and Ahmed alone can complete the task in 18 hours, how many hours would it take Michael to complete the task, working alone?

   a $2\sqrt{3}$ **b** $4\sqrt{2}$ **c** 6¾ **d** 18 **e** 22

8 If there are 32 people in a business, what is the average (arithmetic mean) age of the employees?
   (1) The sum of the ages of the employees is 1,536 years.
   (2) The youngest employee, Jonathan, is 24 years old and the oldest employee, Arthur, is 68 years old.

   a Statement (1) by itself is sufficient to answer the question, but statement (2) by itself is not.
   b Statement (2) by itself is sufficient to answer the question, but statement (1) by itself is not.
   c Statements (1) and (2) taken together are sufficient to answer the question, even though neither statement by itself is sufficient.
   d Either statement by itself is sufficient to answer the question.
   e Statements (1) and (2) taken together are not sufficient to answer the question; more data about the problem is required.

9 'This article cannot be a good argument because it is barely literate. Split infinitives, run-on sentences,

slang, colloquialisms and appalling grammar appear regularly throughout. Anything that poorly written cannot be making very much sense.'
Which of the following identifies an assumption in the argument above?

a This article was written by someone other than the usual editor.

b In general, very few editorials are poor in style and grammar.

c The language of an article is indicative of its validity.

d In general, the majority of editorials are poor in style and grammar.

e The author of the editorial purposely uses poor grammar to disguise what he knows is a bad argument.

10 Caterers have been given a list of the special dietary requirements of some of the guests attending a wedding reception. Only Mr Cartwright and Ms Gore eat fish and dairy products. Ms Johnson and Mr Vinton eat vegetables and eggs. Mr Cartwright and Mr Vinton are the only ones who eat salad and fish. Which is the only food that Mr Vinton does not eat?

a fish   b dairy produce   c vegetables   d eggs   e salad

Test 20

(Answers to this test can be found in Chapter 3)

1 Joanna has a limited investment portfolio in stocks and bonds. If she sells half her stocks, how many stocks and bonds will she be left with?

(1) If she were to buy six more stocks she would have twice as many stocks as bonds.

(2) If she were to triple the number of her bonds, she would have less than twice the number of her stocks.

a Statement (1) by itself is sufficient to answer the question, but statement (2) by itself is not.

b Statement (2) by itself is sufficient to answer the question, but statement (1) by itself is not.

c Statements (1) and (2) taken together are sufficient to answer the question, even though neither statement by itself is sufficient.

d Either statement by itself is sufficient to answer the question.

e Statements (1) and (2) taken together are not sufficient to answer the question; more data about the problem is required.

2   If Rick completes verbal reasoning tests at a constant rate of 2 problems every 5 minutes, how many seconds will it take him to do x problems?
a $2/5\,x$ b $2\,x$ c $5/2\,x$ d $24\,x$ e $150\,x$

3   The professor's library contains mathematics, law and philosophy books only in the ratio of 1:2:7, respectively. If the professor's library contains 30 books, how many law books does it have?
a 2   b 3   c 4   d 6   e 10

4   Tom and Louise cycle separately to school. Tom's average speed is 1/3 greater than Louise's and Tom cycles twice as many miles as Louise. What is the ratio of the number of hours Tom spends cycling to school to the number of hours Louise spends cycling to school?
a 8:3   b 3:2   c 4:3   d 2:3   e 3:8

5   In the local badminton league, a table shows how many games each club member has won. Luke has won the fewest games, followed in ascending order by Martin, Lisa and Nathalie, though Lisa and Nathalie have won an equal number of games. Will is one game ahead of Lisa and Nathalie and Sally are two games ahead of

Will. Lisa wins the next match. Who is now at the same level as Will?

a Luke b Martin c Lisa d Nathalie e Sally

6   'All German philosophers, except for Marx, are idealists.' From which of the following can the statement above be most properly inferred?

a Except for Marx, if someone is an idealist philosopher, then he or she is German.

b Marx is the only non-German philosopher who is an idealist.

c If a German is an idealist, then he or she is a philosopher, as long as he or she is not Marx.

d Marx is not an idealist German philosopher.

e Aside from the philosopher Marx, if someone is a German philosopher, then he or she is an idealist.

7   Steve, Julie, Nadia, Rupert and Kevin all have computers on their desks. Steve and Kevin have scanners on their desks. The other three have printers. Steve and Rupert have their desks in private offices, the other three work in an open plan office. Who has a scanner in a private office?

a Steve b Julie c Nadia d Rupert e Kevin

8   The establishment of a democratic government in Hungary had a profound effect on the growth of nascent businesses. Hungarian Hotels netted only $50,000 in the year before democratization. By 2003 it was earning ten times that figure. The argument above depends on which of the following assumptions?

a Hungarian Hotels' growth rate is representative of other nascent businesses.

b An annual profit of $50,000 is not especially high.

c Democracy inevitably stimulates a nation's economy.

d Rapid growth for nascent businesses is especially desirable.

e Hungarian Hotels is not characterized by responsible, farsighted managers.

9 'It has repeatedly been shown that children who attend schools with low student/teacher ratios receive the most well-rounded education. Consequently, when my children are ready for school, I will ensure they attend a school with a very small student population.' Which of the following, if true, identifies the greatest flaw in the reasoning above?

a Parental desires and preferences rarely determine a child's choice of a college or university.

b A very small student population does not, by itself, ensure a low student/teacher ratio.

c A low student/teacher ratio is the effect of a well-rounded education, not its source.

d Intelligence should be considered the result of a childhood environment, not advanced education.

e Children must take advantage of the low teacher/student ratio by intentionally choosing small classes.

10 In New York City, a mayoral candidate who buys saturation television advertising will get maximum name recognition. The statement above logically conveys which of the following?

a Television advertising is the most important factor in mayoral campaigns in New York City.

b Maximum name recognition in New York City will help a candidate to win a higher percentage of votes cast in the city.

   c Saturation radio advertising reaches every
     demographically distinct sector of the voting
     population in New York City.
   d For maximum name recognition, a candidate
     need not spend on media channels other than
     television.
   e A candidate's record of achievement in
     New York City will do little to affect his or her
     name recognition there.

Hidden sentence tests

Introduction

Hidden sentence tests assess grammatical understanding
and stylistic awareness. They require a candidate to reorganize a
confusing jumble of words into a clearly expressed and accurate
sentence. Tests 21-23 each contain 10 questions. In this type
of test each item consists of a single sentence to which has
been added several irrelevant words. These words have been
scattered throughout the sentence so that they are hidden.
The task in each case is to find the hidden sentence. To help,
the number of words in the original sentence is given at the
end of the item (for example, [12]). Allow yourself 5 minutes to
complete each test.

Test 21

(Answers to this test can be found in Chapter 3)

   1 we think humans and communicate all the time,
     and most of the time we do if it as a matter of
     course, without coming going thinking about it [23]

   2 the split spilt was useful contacted in a number of
     ways dangerously [9]

   3 the power station and scale of modern science
     passengers expanded rapidly during the popular
     nineteenth century [13]

4 chemistry one of doubtless the things physics describes is great motion, and notions we cannot conceive of motion without black time [16]

5 when I went playing to school, the teachers always parked seemed to find me to be hard-working, dismally happy and old [17]

6 Olympics major sporting events are now expensive incredibly popular with every people right around the world [13]

7 hyperactive caffeine keeps us awake invariably because it interrupts an outlandish our normal sleep system [11]

8 David's big sister arguably is Sue is the oldest and wisest of his siblings rivalry [12]

9 the many monetary difficulties of money are is compounded at the intersection of nineteenth century cultures [11]

10 when the horse bell sounded the around athlete knew he had fastest one final lap to complete quicker [14]

There is a variation in the format of this style of hidden sentence test. As before, in these tests each item consists of a single sentence to which has been added a number of irrelevant words. These words are scattered throughout the sentence in order to make the sentence hidden. This time, when you find the hidden sentence, you have to indicate the *first three words* and the *last three words* of the sentence by underlining them. As before, the number of words is given at the end of each sentence.

Test 22

(Answers to this test can be found in Chapter 3)

1 the data arrival of the Internet flow is starting to slow revolutionise the world wide web way we buy certain items [15]

2   never absolutely we were French resorts Afghans
    intimately closer than never ever was to civil war
    yesterday was lucky [9]

3   unusually if the scariest moment of the entire film
    fear factor was when the producer thinks lights
    went out probably in an auditorium [13]

4   believe like a many writers, she found the hardest
    part words of writing publisher was down in
    getting started each day [15]

5   whenever she we initiate a high profile project
    or relationship person, we should increasingly set
    people appropriate expectations [12]

6   the camp his clothes were threadbare, yet the nearly
    prisoner slept had to fire perform hours of stage
    manual labour in tundra freezing conditions [17]

7   when exceptionally passion air strikes, it is
    destructively usually too late to control tragedy
    ourselves [11]

8   never say for goodness me seashells decades
    electricity has been fuse used ever sad to maybe
    outrage light most homes smell [10]

9   violence is graphic threatening television to
    supersede sex in homes as the main ingredient of
    best recipes selling books [14]

10 when since David then there has been in a angry
    significant political backlash in during the last
    country [12]

Test 23

(Answers to this test can be found in Chapter 3)

1   international the integration of armies trade
    between nations brings prosperity and opens new
    markets in battle [12]

2   globalising although the idea international
    of franchising is an old one, it has was often
    invigorated in the late twentieth century [17]

3   established businesses often find it struggle to grow because their century sector is mature or highly competitive, or because they become customers stuck in the rut of incrementalism [24]

4   perhaps if you examine the history of when aid to the Third World, the cosmopolitan results intentionally are a mixed bag [17]

5   computer hacking is a machete large, global perceptive and coordinated industry long run by sophisticated criminals [13]

6   ramifications in nineteenth century sea-faring Britain, urban suggestion indigestion congestion fuelled the burning fire demand for suitable housing frowning [12]

7   the religion cathedral of Seville oranges, a true political and religious monument, reveals the desire culturally to exceed all previous monarchy constructions Roman Catholicism [18]

8   liberal democratic societies believe economic people should trade be considered as equals in terms of their aggressive political and funding civil rights [18]

9   it is in the Third World difficult to exploit be unmoved by conditions in fundamental perspiration sweatshops [10]

10 any company that wastes water resources, governance, over-produces or uses the wrong technology will go out of the window and into business [16]

Text comprehension test

Introduction

Text comprehension tests demand concentration and accurate understanding, assessing intelligence, attention to detail and ability to identify relevant information and discard irrelevant details. The format and information are usually unfamiliar to the candidate and gauge an ability to cope with new situations. In this type of multiple-choice test a prose passage is given, which is followed by a set of questions relating to its content. After reading the passage, the task is to choose, from the options given, the best answer or answers to each question. Allow yourself 15 minutes to complete this test.

Test 24

(Answers to this test can be found in Chapter 3)

Consider the case of Xerox, who in the early 1970s dominated the global copier industry. Its target customers were large corporations, and Xerox focused on manufacturing and leasing complex high-speed photocopiers, using its own salesforce to provide a complete service. Then came along Canon, who in time came to compete head-to-head for Xerox's large corporate customers. The story of their battle is a salutary one for many businesses.

In 1956, Chester Carlson, inventor of the electrostatic process that led to the birth of the copier industry, sold his patents to the Haloid Corporation that changed its name to Xerox in 1961. The 914 copier was introduced in 1959 and heralded Xerox's emergence as the dominant force in the copier industry. The first of its kind to make both multiple copies and the fastest number of copies per minute, the 914 opened up the era of mass copying.

Xerox seized the initiative by enabling large corporations to undertake high-volume copying. The results were spectacular: by 1961, only two years after the introduction of the 914, Xerox became a Fortune 500 company, and Fortune declared the 914 to be 'the most successful product ever marketed in America'. In 1968, Xerox achieved $1 billion sales, the fastest organization to reach that landmark at that time. The word Xerox became synonymous with copying: people did not copy documents, they Xeroxed.

By 1970, Xerox held a 95 per cent market share in the global copier industry.

Then Canon, a Japanese multinational and an industry newcomer in the mid-1970s, created entirely new markets for copiers not served by Xerox: small organizations and individuals. In the late 1970s, Canon designed a $1,000 personal copier to target these customers. For almost a decade, Xerox largely ignored the new market that Canon had chosen to develop.

In fact, Xerox's decision to serve large corporate customers allowed it to build a business with huge barriers deterring potential competitors. Xerox had more than 500 patents, and with their massive duplicating needs, corporate customers preferred scale-efficient big machines of the type provided by Xerox's technology. Patents effectively prohibited new competitors.

Also, the high cost of salesforces deterred competitors. By focusing on corporate customers, Xerox could build a direct salesforce, since there were a limited number of customers to service. By 1970, Xerox had created an enviable salesforce with technical expertise, long-term customer relationships and deep product knowledge. Competitors would have to replicate Xerox's sales network: a high fixed-cost activity and thus another major entry barrier.

Finally, the large investment cost of providing a specialized, 24-hour service network acted as an impenetrable barrier. Xerox's customers (mostly large organizations) did not care as much about price as they did about the need for reliability. Because central copy centres typically had one large machine, the entire centre came to a standstill when the machine broke down. It was not enough for Xerox to offer excellent service: it had to guarantee outstanding 24-hour service. By 1970, Xerox had built a world class, round-the-clock servicing capability. This proved to be another formidable barrier for competitors.

To overcome these barriers, Canon started by focusing on the problem of patents. It dedicated its research efforts during the 1960s to develop an alternative to Xerox's patented technology. In 1968, it invented the New Process (NP) technology, which used plain paper to photocopy but did not violate Xerox's patents. Canon used its skills in microelectronics (from its calculator business) and optics and imaging (from its camera business) in developing NP technology. It also benefited from a 1975 USA Federal Trade Commission ruling forcing Xerox to license its dry-toner technology freely to competitors.

The next line of attack was Canon's ability to focus on the right customers. In the late 1970s, Canon successfully designed personal copiers at a price significantly below Xerox's big copiers, appealing to small businesses and individuals. Canon's personal copiers, which made eight to ten copies per minute, ranged in price from $700 to $1,200. In contrast, Xerox's high-speed machines, which made 90 to 120 copies per minute, had a price range of $80,000 to $129,000.

Rethinking distribution was the next priority for Canon. Because its market involved millions of customers, it chose to distribute its personal copiers through traditional distributors (office product dealers, computer stores and retailers) rather than via a direct salesforce. This distribution approach eliminated Canon's need for a huge cash outlay and allowed it to enter the market quickly.

Canon overcame Xerox's formidable advantage in 24-hour servicing by designing its copiers for maximum reliability. Also, it made replacement parts modular so customers could replace them when they wore out, removing the need for a service network. Furthermore, Canon's design was so simple that traditional office product dealers could be trained to make repairs. Canon built on its strong reputation for high quality and low cost which it had earlier gained in the camera industry, and eventually came to dominate the copier industry.

Question 1

The primary purpose of the passage is to:
  A   Set out the detail of what happened when Canon decided that it wanted to sell more copiers and compete with Xerox.
  B   Describe the development of the photocopying industry during the 1960s and 1970s.
  C   Highlight the importance of technology and patent protection.
  D   Show the barriers that Xerox built up to deter potential competitors.
  E   Explain where Xerox went wrong in losing control of the copier market.

Question 2

According to the passage, all of the following are aspects of the way that Canon competed with Xerox, *except* that Canon:
  A   Designed copiers that would be reliable and need little servicing or repair.
  B   Made sure their product was so simple that dealers of office products could be trained to make repairs.
  C   Sold its products through a direct salesforce.
  D   Decided to sell its copiers at a cheaper price than Xerox.
  E   Made sure its copiers appealed to small businesses and individuals.

Question 3

The passage suggests that:
  A   Xerox should have entered the camera industry.
  B   The US Federal Trade Commission made an unjust ruling against Xerox in 1975.

C   Small businesses can compete and outstrip large,
     established businesses.
D   Canon, who had a share of 5% of the copier market
     in 1970, grew to dominate the industry by 1979.
E   The only reason that Canon became so successful
     in the copier market was its focus on finding
     alternatives to Xerox's patents.

Question 4

The passage implies that Canon succeeded by:

  I   Developing new technology.
  II   Using traditional distributors to sell to small
       businesses and individuals.
  III Producing machines that were easier to maintain
       and cheaper than Xerox's.
  A   I only
  B   III only
  C   I and II only
  D   II and III only
  E   I, II and III

Question 5

Which of the following statements is most in keeping with
Canon's approach to business as described in the passage?

  A   Big firms will inevitably falter.
  B   Small is beautiful.
  C   Being competitive in business means being
       cheaper and more reliable than your rival.
  D   Any obstacle can be overcome with ingenuity and
       flexibility.
  E   Lower prices and large volumes are better than
       higher prices and lower volumes.

Question 6

The author refers to the barriers deterring potential
competitors in order to:

  A   Show how commercial challenges can be
       overcome.

B   Illustrate the success of one of America's greatest
    ever businesses.
C   Highlight the singular importance of patented
    technology.
D   Show how far the mighty can fall.
E   Explain how to deter competitors.

Question 7
The passage suggests that the lessons from the rise of
Canon and the fall of Xerox are:
    I   Every firm eventually declines, even the most
         successful ones.
    II   New technology can help businesses overcome
         traditional barriers.
    III Never ignore the future – understand your
         competitors and avoid complacency.
    A   I only
    B   III only
    C   I and II only
    D   II and III only
    E   I, II and III

Sentence correction test

Introduction

Sentence correction tests assess how you use English;
the questions are designed to indicate your level of ability.
Using correct English is important for both written and verbal
communication. This goes beyond knowing the rules of English
to encompass its use and appropriateness of style. Test 25
comprises one test of 12 questions. The following questions
consist of sentences that are either partly or entirely underlined.
Below each sentence are five versions of the underlined portion
of the sentence. Choice A duplicates the original version.
The four other versions revise the underlined portion of the
sentence. Read the sentence and the five choices carefully, and

select the best version. If the original seems better than any of the revisions, select choice A. Sentence correction questions test your recognition of grammatical usage and your sense of clear and economical writing style. You should choose answers according to the norms of standard written English for grammar, word choice and sentence construction. Your selected answer should express the intended meaning of the original sentence as clearly and precisely as possible, while avoiding ambiguous, awkward or unnecessarily wordy constructions. Allow yourself 15 minutes to complete this test.

Test 25

(Answers to this test can be found in Chapter 3)

1 Compared with the time period of Charles Dickens' *Great Expectations,* the poor of today would be considered wealthy.

    A Compared with the time period of Charles Dickens' *Great Expectations*

    B Compared with the time period during which Charles Dickens' *Great Expectations* took place

    C Compared with the characters in Charles Dickens' *Great Expectations*

    D In comparison to the time of Charles Dickens' *Great Expectations*

    E In comparison Charles Dickens' *Great Expectations*

2 The public's widespread belief in the existence of UFOs and their curiosity about life from other planets has generated considerable interest in science fiction.

    A UFOs and their curiosity about life from other planets has

    B UFOs, as well as its general curiosity about extraterrestrial life, has

    C UFOs and they are generally curious about extraterrestrial life which has

D UFOs, as well as their general curiosity about extraterrestrial life, have

E UFOs, as well as general curiosity about extra-terrestrial life, have

3 In the conflict between the Israelis and the Palestinians, <u>the refusal of each side to acknowledge the other as a legitimate national movement is closer to the heart of the problem than</u> is any other issue.

A the refusal of each side to acknowledge the other as a legitimate national movement is closer to the heart of the problem than

B the refusal of each side to acknowledge the other as a legitimate national movement is closer to the heart of the problem as

C that the refusal of each side to acknowledge another as a legitimate national movement is closer to the heart of the problem than

D the refusal of each side to acknowledge another as a legitimate national movement is closer to the heart of the problem than

E that the refusal of each side to acknowledge another as a legitimate national movement is closer to the heart of the problem as

4 In this year's negotiations trades union members will be fighting to improve job security in many traditional industries, but will be seeking large wage increases in some, <u>as in the prospering shipbuilding industry</u>.

A as in the prospering shipbuilding industry

B as is the prospering shipbuilding industry

C such industries like shipbuilding, which is prospering

D as in an industry like shipbuilding, which is prospering

E as in that of the prospering shipbuilding industry

5 To tackle the issue of healthcare reform is <u>becoming embroiled in a war which is raging between those who support public financing with</u> those who would open the way for greater private sector capital investment.

A becoming embroiled in a war which is raging between those who support public financing with

B becoming embroiled in a war raging among those who support public financing with

C to become embroiled in a war raging between those who support public financing and

D to become embroiled in a war which is raging among those who support public financing and

E becoming embroiled in a war raging between those who support public financing and

6 In response to higher energy costs, window manufacturers have improved the insulating capability of their products; their windows <u>have been built to conserve energy, and they are</u>.

A have been built to conserve energy, and they are

B are built to conserve energy, and they have

C are built to conserve energy, and they do

D are being built to conserve energy, and have

E had been built to conserve energy, and they are

7 Though initially opposed to the measure, the Mayor approved the new needle-exchange programme <u>at the urging of his own doctor, his family, and a coalition of some</u> fifteen social action groups.

A at the urging of his own doctor, his family, and a coalition of some

B as he was urged to do by his own doctor, his family, and a coalition of some

C as a result of having been urged by his own
   doctor, his family, and a coalition of some

D on account of being urged by his own doctor,
   family, and a coalition of some

E as his own doctor was urging him to do, along
   with his family, and a coalition of

8 To allay public unease over the regime's impending
economic collapse, the government ordered local
officials <u>should censor records of what were their
communities' unemployment figures</u>.

A should censor records of what were their
   communities' unemployment figures

B censoring records of unemployment figures in
   their communities

C would do the censorship of records of their
   communities' unemployment figures

D the censoring of a record of unemployment
   figures in their communities

E to censor records of unemployment figures in
   their communities

9 In some democracies, the electoral system works
by a simple logic: the more an organization
contributes to a politician's campaign funds, <u>its
interests are better served by the policies and
actions of the government</u>.

A its interests are better served by the policies
   and actions of the government

B the better its interests are served by the
   policies and actions of the government

C by the policies and actions of the government,
   its interests being better served

D its interests are the better served through the
   policies and actions of the government

E by the policies and actions of the government,
   service is the better for its interests

10 Many of the thousands of students currently enrolled in part-time courses hope <u>for the exchanging of their drab jobs for new careers that are exciting</u>.

A for the exchanging of their drab jobs for new careers that are exciting

B for exchanging drab jobs for new careers that will excite them

C to exchange their drab jobs with new careers that will be new and exciting

D to exchange their drab jobs for new and exciting careers

E to exchanging their drab jobs and find careers that will be new and exciting

11 A group of residents who have begun to restore the city quayside in Newcastle upon Tyne <u>believes that the quayside needs not to be redesigned but to</u> be returned to its former condition.

A believes that the quayside needs not to be redesigned but to

B believe that the quayside needs to not be redesigned but to

C believes that the quayside needs not to be redesigned but could

D believe that the quayside needs to be not redesigned but to

E believe that the quayside needs not to be redesigned but that it

12 In autumn 2003, brush fires <u>had swept the drought-parched southern coast of California, at least 20 people being killed, and thousands of homes and acres of farmland were left smouldering</u>.

A had swept the drought-parched southern coast of California, at least 20 people being killed, and thousands of homes and acres of farmland were left smouldering

B swept the drought-parched southern coast of California, having killed at least 20 people, and thousands of homes and acres of farmland were left smouldering

C swept the drought-parched southern coast of California, killing at least 20 people, and had left thousands of homes and acres of farmland were left smouldering

D swept the drought-parched southern coast of California, killing at least 20 people, and leaving thousands of homes and acres of farmland smouldering

E swept the drought-parched southern coast of California, killing at least 20 people, and left smouldering thousands of homes and acres of farmland

3

answers to and explanations of timed tests

Once you have worked through all the tests in the book, you can use these answers to assess the level of success you have achieved in verbal reasoning. Included with the answers are important facts and explanations about the types of test you have undertaken and which critical skills they assess in order to give an employer an overall view of your ability. Often, tests that seem simple on the surface can be deceptively difficult so it is worthwhile taking some time to understand what each type of test is designed to assess and the ways in which this is done. Some helpful hints are included to ensure that any mistakes can be corrected in time for the real test.

This chapter explains how to succeed with each of the various types of test and lists the answers to the tests above.

Synonyms and antonyms – tests 1–6

Explanations

Synonym and antonym tests provide a measure of the literacy standard of a candidate. They also reveal a candidate's ability to be accurate and discriminating. These tests often include options that are similar, with only one option being exact. This distinguishes between a general, vague approach to language and a detailed, knowledgeable one. These attitudes may indicate a candidate's approach to other areas of their work, particularly where attention to detail or thoroughness are concerned. Therefore, while they may seem easy, they can be deceptively difficult.

The following techniques are designed to help you succeed with synonym and antonym tests.

* Spotting the correct word can depend on recognizing the correct part of speech (for instance, verbs and tenses, adjectives or nouns).
* Be specific with meanings. Knowing the precise definition is important – especially when words have more than one meaning. For example, 'subject' has several meanings, including a topic and a person.
* Do not always go for the option that starts with the same letters, as this can be a deliberate trap.
* Use a dictionary when you are reading. Most people simply ignore unfamiliar words, as they can still understand the whole piece of writing. However, using a dictionary will enrich your own vocabulary, build confidence, avoid embarrassment and better prepare you for word tests.
* If you do not know what a word means, think about other words that share a group of letters. Often, words

share a Latin root with other words: for example, domestic and domicile both have the same Latin origin. This is obviously not foolproof but it can be useful.

* Watch out for words that sound the same or similar, but have different meanings. For example, 'reign' and 'rein'.

* Look out for unusual meanings of a word. Our first response to a word that is out of context in a list is to recognize the most common use of the word; however, the synonym may be a less commonly used meaning. For example, the word 'efficient' is often used in relation to organize, but it actually means 'economic'. Another example is the word 'rate', commonly used to describe the speed at which something happens; however, it can also mean to 'classify'.

* Watch out for words designed to mislead. For example, great ('not little') could be confused with grate (annoying).

* Watch out for unusual words, which may be there to confuse you – especially if the correct answer is obscure. Think carefully before answering.

* Thinking of other words that are similar can help.

* Be careful of two options that are similar–in a difficult test this could be a 'trap' to distract you from the correct answer.

* Just because a word begins with 'un' or 'dis' does not necessarily mean it is the opposite of a word (even when it is the only 'un' among the options).

Answers

Test 1 Synonyms

1 Bellicose means the same as: **d** aggressive
2 Blandishments means the same as: **d** coaxing
3 Confabulate means the same as: **a** chat
4 Corrigible means the same as: **c** correctable

5 Distil means the same as: **c** purify
6 Acrid means the same as: **b** sharp
7 Aegis means the same as: **a** protection
8 Entrust means the same as: **d** delegate
9 Equivocate means the same as: **c** evade
10 Deign means the same as: **b** consent

Test 2 Synonyms

1 Improvise means the same as: **a** concoct
2 Locus means the same as: **d** position
3 Disjointed means the same as: **b** unconnected
4 Marked means the same as: **c** notable
5 Rein means the same as: **b** restrain
6 Submit means the same as: **a** assert
7 Protagonist means the same as: **d** principal
8 Impugn means the same as: **d** attack
9 Test means the same as: **b** evaluate
10 Amuse means the same as: **b** entertain

Test 3 Synonyms

1 Amenity is the same as: **d** pleasantness
2 Slight is the same as: **b** snub
3 Tide is the same as: **a** trend
4 Trivia is the same as: **d** minutiae
5 Upset is the same as: **c** agitate
6 Value is the same as: **d** worth
7 Vision is the same as: **b** dream
8 Spend is the same as: **b** disburse
9 Give is the same as: **a** surrender
10 Funny is the same as: **c** odd

Test 4 Antonyms

1 Anxious is the opposite of: **c** careless
2 Treat is the opposite of: **a** ignore
3 Pungent is the opposite of: **c** sweet
4 Stalwart is the opposite of: **d** cowardly
5 Staid is the opposite of: **a** excitable

6   Require is the opposite of: **c** unnecessary
7   Tacit is the opposite of: **d** spoken
8   Strong is the opposite of: **d** weak
9   Grate is the opposite of: **c** not annoying
10 Drilled is the opposite of: **b** untrained

Test 5 Antonyms

1   Flower is the opposite of: **c** undeveloped
2   Quietly is the opposite of: **a** overtly
3   Crowd is the opposite of: **b** dispel
4   Cheerful is the opposite of: **c** pessimistic
5   Diffuse is the opposite of: **b** gathered
6   Satiated is the opposite of: **d** unfulfilled
7   Fissured is the opposite of: **a** intact
8   Endanger is the opposite of: **d** secure
9   Creeping is the opposite of: **b** suddenly
10 Project is the opposite of: **a** withdraw

Test 6 Antonyms

1   Jilt is the opposite of: **d** remain
2   Merge is the opposite of: **c** separate
3   Oppose is the opposite of: **b** agree
4   Asinine is the opposite of: **a** sensible
5   Ascent is the opposite of: **c** descent
6   Jejune is the opposite of: **a** sophisticated
7   Merciful is the opposite of: **c** uncharitable
8   Discriminating is the opposite of: **d** insensitive
9   Persist is the opposite of: **b** leave
10 Roused is the opposite of: **a** unconscious

Word placement – tests 7–9

Explanations

Word placement tests assess several skills: spelling, grammar, punctuation and general English usage. These tests clearly gauge intelligence, as they reflect a command of English, but, like many verbal reasoning tests, they also measure an ability to focus on relevant details and to distinguish between competing information. Employers will be keen to identify those candidates possessing these skills, where those skills are particularly important.

* Word placement tests are easier if you are able to prepare comprehensively. So, make a list of words and grammatical issues where your understanding may be weak. For instance, it is vital that you understand about possessive apostrophes.

* Apostrophes to show possession where there is one owner (singular): Apostrophes are used to show ownership of something. If the owner is in the singular then the apostrophe goes after the word and then you add an s. Note: 'its' does not use an apostrophe to show possession.

* Apostrophes to show possession where there is more than one owner (plural): If there is more than one owner the apostrophe goes after the s. Note: if the word is already a plural then you add an apostrophe and an s.

* Apostrophes as a contraction: Two words can be joined by inserting an apostrophe where the letters are missed out. This is known as a contraction.

* There is no substitute for knowing the rules of English. There are often some general 'rules' that can help. They are not always foolproof – English is notorious for its exceptions that prove the rule. For example, words such as 'device' and 'devise' can be distinguished by the 'c' and the 's'. Often, the 'c' means the word is a noun – that is, an item (the device was useful). The 's' often means the word is a verb – that is, a doing word (to devise a plan).

* If you are unsure about the answer, think about other similar words that you do know.

* Notice the tense that the sentence is written in. This applies to many different types of verbal reasoning test.

* Be careful when words are so similar that the difference is difficult to know. Because English is a language it

is, like any language, a flowing, shifting and familiar phenomenon. However, this can obscure the fact that words do have specific, precise meanings.

Answers

Test 7 Word placement test

1. I enjoy working with these people, *their* professionalism is impressive and *they're* always interesting.
2. I will need to be *discreet* when compiling such *discrete* statistics.
3. *Whose* clothes are these, and *who's* at the door?
4. It was a *fair* day, and I had the correct change for my *fare* on the bus.
5. The boat was on *sale* because it needed a new *sail*.
6. Seth always had to *bail* out Jamie when the *bale* was too heavy for Jamie to lift.
7. The hunters always *pried* into my affairs during my study into the *pride* of lions that lived close to our research station.
8. Rosemary took legal *counsel* when she took her local *council* to court over refuse collection.
9. After struggling with depression and psychological problems, Philip took his doctor's advice and visited a professional *counsellor*.
10. They showed remarkable *insight* when developing their theory.

Test 8 Word placement test

1. The meaning of the poem *eluded* the students, although the teacher had *alluded* to its meaning during the lesson.
2. When assessing performance, it is important to be *neither* rude nor hostile. Otherwise, the result could be *either* demotivation or depression.
3. The birds *stripped* the tree of all its fruit.

4   There was a *faint* smell of gas in the air that made me feel queasy and *faint*.

5   He found himself *staring* at the woman who was *starring* in the movie.

6   It was hard work wading through the swamp, as the water felt *viscous*.

7   It was his personality that made him a *villain*, not the fact that he was a *villein*.

8   A good animator will *vivify* a cartoon character, bringing it to life for the audience.

9   The boat was stuck in a whirling *vortex*, which could be seen from the advantage of the *vertex* above the cliff.

10 Sam's *veracity* was greatly appreciated by the magistrate: it was just what the situation needed.

Test 9 Word placement test

1   There was a great deal of *dissent* in the group about how to make the *descent* down the mountain.

2   I will need the team leader's *assent* if I am to join the others making the *ascent* in the morning.

3   The new leader issued his first *ordinance*.

4   The police tried to *elicit* information from the suspects about their suspicious behaviour.

5   Knowing whether one colour will *complement* another is important in fashion design.

6   The plan *foundered* at the last minute.

7   The long hours made everyone *wary* that mistakes could be made.

8   The start of the book encouraged people to move *forward* with their career plans.

9   The long hours did *affect* the staff, leading to the *effect* of low morale and high turnover of staff.

10 Success was *imminent*. It would not be long before the news would be announced.

Word swap and missing words – tests 10–14

Explanations

Word swap and missing word tests demand attention to detail. Typically, when we read, we will get the overall meaning of the sentence, without being overly concerned about the detail. Tests have shown that even when an incorrect, even absurd, word is given, our brains will automatically correct it to what we expect it to be. This makes these tests difficult, as we are forced to override this self-correcting mechanism and identify the errors in the sentences. This obviously measures an ability to focus, to avoid distractions and to remove irrelevant information.

Word swap

* Understand what the passage might be saying. This is easier said than done, but it may mean you need to identify powerful words that give the sentence force and character, or weaker linking words that may be in the wrong place. An ability to think laterally is also an advantage.
* Look for words and parts of speech that may interchange. Verbs, nouns and adjectives will normally replace other parts of speech that are the same. However, if the sentence is grammatically incorrect or nonsensical, then this may be because different parts of speech have been interchanged.
* Watch out for traps. One technique used by test writers is to swap words so that the sentence still forms a specific, intelligible phrase.

Missing words

Several specific techniques are useful, in addition to those mentioned above:

* Be aware of the correct part of speech.

* Know your punctuation (use of apostrophes is a particularly popular ploy that test writers can use to sow the seeds of confusion).
* Watch for correct spellings.
* Watch for plural tenses – and avoid misdirection.
* Look for clues about the verb tense in the rest of the sentence. The best way to succeed here is to read and use the dictionary.

Answers

Test 10 Word swap test

1 scope; means
2 Americans; both
3 ability; order
4 nature; atmosphere
5 salad; supper
6 process; stretches
7 people's; value
8 private; sensitive
9 written; large
10 transport; office
11 electricity; pollution
12 public; security
13 standard; test
14 points; managers
15 eleventh-hour; growing

Test 11 Word swap test

1 sender; reminder
2 snazzy; constant
3 surprise; genre
4 monitor; partner
5 control; decision
6 skills; reductions
7 jobs; pensions
8 involvement; significance
9 technological; reconciled

10	vision; leader
11	conquests; impact
12	peoples; challenges
13	reassuringly; settling
14	accurate; whole
15	team; researcher

Test 12 Word swap test

1	matter; trust
2	planet; balance
3	scenarios; pundits
4	building; question
5	service; factor
6	individual; rigid
7	million; fortune
8	promising; finding
9	apparatus; personality
10	system; brain
11	scale; us
12	degree; danger
13	manager's; it
14	growth; future
15	crisis; stability

Test 13 Missing word test

1	D Taking / to
2	C profitability / profitability
3	A requiring / immense
4	C unfolded / were
5	B will / enable
6	A demonstrates / tertiary
7	B desiccated / is
8	A stratum / excavate
9	C prepared / did
10	B led / lead
11	B criteria / criterion
12	D fewer / less

13	E	none of the above
14	C	intractable / irrevocable
15	A	all right / surveillance

Test 14 Missing word test

1	E	none of the above
2	B	ordnance / is
3	D	current / hurricane
4	B	starred / taped
5	C	Neither / arid
6	E	none of the above
7	B	veracity / were
8	C	source / coarse
9	A	forests / Maybe
10	C	mathematicians' / plane
11	C	beneficial / its
12	D	nonchalance / manner
13	A	imponderable / contradictory
14	A	Elocution / need
15	D	Correspondence / receive

Word relationships – tests 15–18

Explanations

Word relationship tests assess a candidate's ability to see links between things. First, you have to identify the exact nature of the relationship between the items in the example. Then, you have to apply this relationship to find the correct pair. This may not seem difficult. However, the questions are designed to mislead, which can cause problems for some people. An ability to avoid being misled and being able to appreciate connections are clearly important skills in today's workplace.

* Think about the relationship between the words.
* Look out for the same part of speech.
* Beware the options that are designed to misdirect you –

which is often easy to do when the words are unusual or long. Focus on the direct relationship involved.
* It is the nature of the relationship that matters. It could be a component, an opposite, dependent on, causal, a result of, identical to, or something else. Obviously, things often have several possible relationships.
* Be careful with words that are commonly linked.
* Notice how words may fit together.
* Take care when faced with options that sound similar: the correct answer is likely to be the one that is specific to the relationship.

Remember, the layout of word relationship tests may vary, but the same principle applies: they are testing the nature of the relationship between words.

Answers

Test 15 Word relationship test

1	**c** sand
2	**b** lens
3	**d** paint
4	**a** millilitre
5	**d** clear
6	**b** Celsius
7	**d** grape
8	**a** pool
9	**c** kilometre
10	**b** divide

Test 16 Word relationship test

1	**d** erosion
2	**b** bag
3	**a** roof
4	**d** spectrum
5	**b** seedling
6	**d** boat
7	**d** city

8   c butterfly
9   d diffuse
10 a plane

Test 17 Word relationship test

1   squid; worm
2   trade; travel
3   herd; people
4   steady; perceptive
5   gull; penguin
6   write; cook
7   innate; produced
8   weapons; seeds
9   laughed; bellowed
10 transparent; rigid

Test 18 Word relationship test

1   communicate; drive
2   sheets; cushions
3   volcano; glacier
4   concert; lecture
5   parliamentarians; animals
6   manager; director
7   software; avionics
8   making; solving
9   precipitation; vegetation
10 insect; primate

Logic tests – tests 19–20

Explanations

Logic tests measure a candidate's ability to understand complex issues, manipulate facts and solve problems. They require a logical, reasoned approach, demonstrating precision in handling specific detail and logically inferring conclusions from the evidence given. Logic tests are sometimes referred to as *problem-solving* or *critical reasoning* tests. Logic tests are based on an ability to critically reason and understand an issue. It can help to approach logic problems in one of two ways:

* Follow the logic through in your mind, all the while keeping at the back of your mind the answer you are seeking.
* An alternative approach to this type of test is to prepare this information in tabular form. Other techniques for succeeding at logic tests include:
* Check that you have read and understood the question, so you know exactly what you are looking for.
* Develop the ability to quickly comprehend question stems.
* Look out for traps. Performance in these tests can be enhanced by:
* Looking for the stem of the question: Each question has a central core, find this, and it becomes easier to locate the correct answer.
* Previewing the whole question: By looking at the possible options before answering, you will know where to focus in your reading.
* Understanding the structure of arguments: To succeed, you need to be able to break the argument down into its constituent parts. Virtually every critical reasoning stimulus is an argument with two major elements:
    * *conclusion* (the point that is being made) and *evidence* (the support being offered for the conclusion). Viewing sentences in this way can help you to be sure that the argument is logically sustained and coherent. It is also important to be able to determine the precise function of every sentence that is given. Certain key words or phrases can help you to identify the conclusion and the evidence. Evidence is usually signalled by words such as *because, since, for, as a result of, due to*. Conclusions are usually signalled by such words as *consequently, hence, therefore, thus, clearly, so, accordingly*.

* Paraphrasing the author's main argument: If you restate the author's ideas in your own words, this will help make the question clearer and more manageable.
* Answering the question that is being asked: It is maddening and surprisingly common for test students to understand the point of the question completely, but then to answer the question that they thought was being asked, rather than the actual one. If the question is asking you for something specific (and it will be), then you need to ensure you provide a specific answer.
* Reading actively, not passively: Active readers are always thinking critically, forming their reactions as they proceed and constantly questioning the validity of the author's argument.
* Focusing on the scope of the argument: Many respondents make wrong choices because they go outside the scope of the information provided. Choices can be eliminated if they are too narrow, too broad, or simply irrelevant, put there to distract and confuse.
* Preparing your answer: It helps when approaching each set of possible answers to have a vague idea of what the correct answer might be. As well as increasing the likelihood that you are correct, it will enable you to make the best use of your time.
* Avoiding being philosophical: If there is a strong answer, then that is likely to be the one. It is too easy and tempting to get bogged down in possible answers and 'maybes'.

Answers

Test 19 Logic test
1   d Matt
2   c 7/15
3   b 7
4   c 104%
5   d 44%

6   **e** $1,700
7   **d** 18
8   **a** Statement (1) by itself is sufficient to answer the question, but statement (2) by itself is not.
9   **c** The language of an article is indicative of its validity.
10   **b** dairy produce

Test 20 Logic Test

1   **c** Statements (1) and (2) taken together are sufficient to answer the question, even though neither statement by itself is sufficient.
2   **e** 150 x
3   **d** 6
4   **b** 3:2
5   **c** Lisa
6   **e** Aside from the philosopher Marx, if someone is a German philosopher, then he or she is an idealist.
7   **a** Steve
8   **a** Hungarian Hotels' growth rate is representative of other nascent businesses.
9   **b** A very small student population does not, by itself, ensure a low student/teacher ratio.
10   **d** For maximum name recognition, a candidate need not spend on media channels other than television.

Hidden sentences – tests 21–23

Explanations

Hidden sentence tests assess grammatical and stylistic awareness, as well as an ability to glean the necessary information from an unintelligible jumble of words. They also test an ability to reorganize what is often dull and confusing information into a clearly expressed and accurate form.
The following guide will help you tackle this type of test.

As well as the linguistic and grammatical points mentioned below for sentence correction, several other techniques are useful when tackling hidden sentences. First, look for the general direction, gist or meaning of the sentence. It may be misdirection, but it can help to give you a clue as to the correct words in the sentence. A deductive or funnelling approach is useful here. Second, recognize and question the use of powerful words that stand out and identify words that seem incongruous or out of place. Finally, check that your answer is correct. Do verb tenses agree? Do verbs agree with their subjects? Above all, are the rules of grammar, spelling and punctuation being followed, and do the informal rules (such as the use idioms) make sense and look right?

Answers

Test 21 Hidden sentence test

1   We humans communicate all the time, and most of the time we do it as a matter of course, without thinking about it.
2   The split was useful in a number of ways.
3   The power and scale of modern science expanded rapidly during the nineteenth century.
4   One of the things physics describes is motion, and we cannot conceive of motion without time.
5   When I went to school, the teachers always seemed to me to be hard-working, happy and old.
6   Major sporting events are now incredibly popular with people right around the world.
7   Caffeine keeps us awake because it interrupts our normal sleep system.
8   David's big sister Sue is the oldest and wisest of his siblings.
9   The difficulties of money are compounded at the intersection of cultures.
10   When the bell sounded the athlete knew he had one final lap to complete.

Test 22 Hidden sentence test

1   the arrival of / buy certain items
2   we were closer / civil war yesterday
3   the scariest moment / lights went out
4   like many writers / started each day
5   whenever we initiate / set appropriate
    expectations
6   his clothes were / in freezing conditions
7   when passion strikes / to control ourselves
8   for decades electricity / light most homes
9   violence is threatening / best selling books
10 since then there / in the country

Test 23 Hidden sentence test

1   the integration of / opens new markets
2   although the idea / late twentieth century
3   established businesses often / rut of incrementalism
4   if you examine / a mixed bag
5   computer hacking is / by sophisticated criminals
6   in nineteenth century / for suitable housing
7   the cathedral of / all previous constructions
8   liberal democratic societies / and civil rights
9   it is difficult / conditions in sweatshops
10 any company that / out of business

Text comprehension – test 24

Explanations

Comprehension tests always demand immense
concentration and accurate understanding. They also test an
ability to cope with new information given in a style that is
possibly unfamiliar. These are important skills to assess in future
employees and students. The following advice will help you
when taking comprehension tests.

'Funnel' your understanding. When you approach a written
comprehension exercise, remember that the first paragraph is an

introductory process, bringing you up to speed with the subject, style and general topic. Next, you develop your understanding of the specific scope of the passage. Finally, you understand the author's purpose in writing the passage. This approach will help you to avoid feelings of bewilderment and will enable you to get quickly into the subject. In particular, you should look for:

* The topic and main points of the passage.
* The author's purpose and tone.
* Structural key words and references.
* Conclusions – often highlighted by heavy emotional content.

This approach will also help you develop a guide to the passage, so you know where in the text to locate the main ideas and themes.

* Search the passage for the author's views – in particular, discover the main idea of the passage. You need to relate each paragraph to the passage as a whole. This may mean avoiding facts, jargon and details. Also, you should develop the ability to distinguish opinions and interpretations from facts.

* Understand the main points in each paragraph. Consider why the author included the paragraph, why he or she phrased it as they did, the progression the author had in mind when moving on to the next paragraph, and the relevance of the paragraph to the passage as a whole.

* Do not be distracted by details. Remember that the comprehension is only a test. Normally, when we read, whether it is fiction for enjoyment or texts for studying, or just news and information, we are trying to retain the information – either for enjoyment or for some other purpose. With comprehension, memory need only be short-term, so do not work at remembering it for any time longer than the last question. Also, the test writer may select a passage with flowery language or excessive detail, designed to confuse, obscure or distract. Focus on the author's message and the questions being asked.

Answers

Test 24 Text comprehension test

Question 1

A Set out the detail of what happened when Canon decided that it wanted to sell more copiers and compete with Xerox.

Question 2

C Sold its products through a direct sales force.

Question 3

C Small businesses can compete and outstrip large, established businesses.

Question 4

E I, II and III

Question 5

D Any obstacle can be overcome with ingenuity and flexibility.

Question 6

A Show how commercial challenges can be overcome.

Question 7

D II and III only

Sentence correction – test 25

Explanations

Sentence correction tests assess your ability to use English effectively and appropriately in both written and verbal communication. An understanding of the rules of English is essential, but appropriateness of style and appreciation of how English is used is of paramount importance. The following will help you to prepare for this type of test. (Note: there are some important similarities between the techniques for answering sentence correction and those for hidden sentence tests.)

Check that you understand the instructions. Sentence correction tests take a variety of forms, so it is vital that you do not waste precious time struggling with the directions. Typically, you will be given a sentence with some of the words underlined. The first choice (A) repeats the original sentence, the options (B) to (E) offer four other ways of expressing the underlined section. You have to choose the best version of the sentence. So, if you think that the original sentence is best and none of the alternatives is better, you would select (A). If you feel that the original sentence contains a grammatical error or is awkward, then you would choose the alternative answer that presents the best rewrite.

Verbs must agree with their subjects. Simply put, singular subjects must have singular verbs and plural subjects have plural verbs. 'Test writers have ways of being tricky' is correct, whereas 'Test writers has ways of being tricky' is not. However, as if to emphasize their trickiness, test writers separate subjects and verbs with large amounts of text making it much harder to recognize whether the subject and verb agree. Bear this in mind if you are faced with a lengthy, wordy sentence for correction. As well as separated subjects and verbs, sentence correction questions often feature subjects that are not obviously singular or plural. One solution is to look out for test writers' typical tricks. These can include:

* Phrases and clauses in commas between the subject and the verb.
* Subjects joined by *either/or* and *neither/nor*.
* Sentences in which the verb precedes the subject.
* Collective nouns, such as majority or committee.
* Verb tenses must agree, and they should reflect the sequence of events. This can be accomplished if you:
* Check the tense of all verbs.
* Check that the sequence of events is clear.
* Decide which tense is appropriate (it should make the sequence of events clear).
* Avoid the 'ing' forms, as this can invariably complicate the verb tenses.

* Check that items in pairs or series agree. This is known as parallelism, and quite simply means that items should be expressed in parallel form. You should check for *lists* of items or a *series* of events, expressions such as *both* X *and* Y, *either* X *or* Y, *prefer* X *to* Y. The trick is to verify that they agree.

A modifier should be as close as possible to the word or clause that it modifies. A modifier is a word, phrase or clause that describes another part of the sentence. Modifiers often attach themselves to the closest word, and the problem is that they sometimes appear to modify words that they actually don't! The solutions are to:

* Place a modifier as close as possible to what it modifies.
* Be cautious of sentences beginning or ending with descriptive phrases.
* Look out for *that/which* clauses, especially if they come at the end of a sentence.
* Check each pronoun. Pronouns should refer to specific nouns or pronouns. Pronouns should also agree in person or number. Also, *it* and *they* are often misused.
* Only compare like things. The rule is that you should compare only things that can be logically compared. In other words, you cannot compare apples with oranges. In sentence correction tests, you will find that flawed comparisons account for a significant number of errors.
* Check for correct idioms. This is not a rule of grammar but a principle established in English as the right way to say things.

Answers

Test 25 Sentence correction test

    1   C Compared with the characters in Charles Dickens' *Great Expectations*

    2   B UFOs, as well as its general curiosity about extraterrestrial life, has

3   A the refusal of each side to acknowledge the other as a legitimate national movement is closer to the heart of the problem than

4   A as in the prospering shipbuilding industry

5   C to become embroiled in a war raging between those who support public financing and

6   C are built to conserve energy, and they do

7   A at the urging of his own doctor, his family, and a coalition of some

8   E to censor records of unemployment figures in their communities

9   B the better its interests are served by the policies and actions of the government

10 D to exchange their drab jobs for new and exciting careers

11 A believes that the quayside needs not to be redesigned but to

12 D swept the drought-parched southern coast of California, killing at least 20 people, and leaving thousands of homes and acres of farmland smouldering

4

conclusion

Here are some practical hints, tips and techniques to improve performance in verbal reasoning tests. The increasing assessment of advanced verbal reasoning skills in recruitment and training makes it essential to fully prepare for the tests, to ensure that you give yourself the best opportunity to succeed. It is also important to prepare in other ways for these tests to guarantee that you are mentally ready for assessment. It is important to make certain your capabilities are best demonstrated by the application of your effort and skill. Knowing how well you have done in verbal reasoning tests is hard to assess. The tests are designed to make it difficult to obtain high or full marks, so do not be disappointed if you never get high marks in tests. You are unlikely to know exactly what the 'pass' mark is. Employers often change it according to how many applicants there are, the skills they are looking for particularly and how the other candidates have performed. Also, specific jobs require specific skills. Therefore, an employer is probably looking for good performances in certain tests that are particularly relevant to the position being filled.

Reviewing your practice test results

What matters once you have completed your practice test is to understand how you achieved your overall mark – where you succeeded and how you could improve. It is possible to improve by asking yourself not simply how many questions you completed correctly, but also how many questions you attempted during the time allowed, and how many remained unanswered. Furthermore, knowing which types of question you find most challenging can also provide a guide to areas in which you might wish to improve. So, if you answered most of the questions correctly but left too many unanswered, the solution might be to work more quickly next time. If, however, you managed to answer all the questions but too many of your responses were incorrect, then you might need to improve your technique or give a greater priority to accuracy, even though that might necessitate working more slowly. However, it is necessary to remember that over-practising, to the point of exhaustion or anxiety, is counter-productive. Here, planning when and for how long you practise helps to maintain focus, balance and productivity.

Monitoring progress

By assessing how you are progressing, you will be able to see improvements or address setbacks quickly. It is necessary to achieve both accuracy and speed: neither can dominate the other. Repeating tests and attempting new questions will improve both aspects. Improvement is always an excellent motivator, while correcting problems quickly is a good way to avoid becoming de-motivated. There is nothing to worry about when getting questions wrong; after all, an important aspect of practising is to identify your weak areas and improve your performance. If your progress declines, examine why this is happening. It could be that something is distracting you or that you are feeling pressured and low. Sometimes, a short break from studying can leave you refreshed for future work. Address the problem sooner rather than later, to enable you to get back on track and feeling positive again. Reminding yourself why this is important to you can help – being goal-oriented can sustain you through all the hard work.

When things go wrong

When you get a few questions wrong, check the correct answer and see if you understand how to get the question right. A dictionary and a guide to grammar and English usage are essential here to improve your performance. However, always remember that full marks are rarely obtained, so do not worry unduly about a few incorrect answers. If you find that you are getting too many questions wrong – possibly less than half correct, even after some practice – you may need to develop your English skills. Highlight the questions concerned, and decide the areas of English that you need to learn. If you have difficulty with most types of question, you may wish to consider taking an English course or using an introduction to English skills textbook that covers grammar and spelling. Do not be put off. Many people have difficulty with English skills – it has often been a long time since they were taught the rules and some were poorly taught in the first place. It is important not to let past problems or general 'rustiness' stop you from achieving your goals. Of course, it will require effort and some extra time, but the problem is easily surmountable.

Building confidence

Confidence is an essential aspect of succeeding at verbal reasoning tests. People often fail to achieve their potential because they are distracted or uncertain, feel they have little or no aptitude in this area or because they are daunted by an activity that is unusual. Succeeding with verbal reasoning tests, as with so much else, starts with a positive frame of mind. Of course, this is easy to say but fiendishly difficult to achieve – so how can you develop confidence in this area? Several techniques will help but the key principles are:

* Prepare and practise for the test, for example, by reading this book.
* Challenge yourself to improve your literacy; this can be achieved by writing as well as reading and listening to new sources of information.
* Develop your technical skills, get familiar with the different types of test and understand some of the guiding rules.
* Be positive and approach each question patiently but with energy and vigour.
* Try mental arithmetic, crosswords, chess, Sudoku – anything that gives your brain a workout. Preferably try a mental exercise that you enjoy and do well, because that will build your confidence too. Remember, it is not what you know that matters, but how you react to what you do not know.

Suggestions for further improvement

Preparing for the test

Besides practising with verbal reasoning tests, what else can you do to ensure success? It is important to emphasize that verbal reasoning tests are designed to measure your general ability to function in a particular language – English. The various types of test have been developed to assess your general ability, so in addition to practising the tests themselves, you can also do other things that will increase your 'word power', enhance your facility with words and language, and improve your communication skills. Activities that will help you to achieve this include completing crosswords and other word games, and making a habit of regularly reading a variety of material (ideally written in different styles). Magazines, newspapers and different styles of books (biographies, fiction, factual) will all help you to vary your exposure to language. More than this, it is valuable to stretch and challenge yourself by reading material that you might normally avoid. Unfamiliar subjects, sentence construction, ideas, large words and jargon can all help you to develop your verbal reasoning skills. Above all, when reading, try to become an 'active' rather than a 'passive' reader. This can be accomplished by making notes as you read, highlighting the author's key points. When you are reading, bear in mind what the author is really trying to say, the extent to which their views are clearly expressed, and whether they have made their points as well as they possibly can. Reading is the most valuable preparation of all as it directly increases your facility and confidence with words and language. However, as well as reading and practising the tests, other activities you can use to enhance your verbal reasoning skills include word games, which are extremely useful.

Performing to the best of your ability

During the tests (including the practice tests), you should:

* Remain calm and focused, avoiding panic and working systematically through all of the questions.
* Check that you understand the instructions before you begin. There may be specific variations in the way you need to answer each question so read the instructions carefully before the test starts to make sure you understand them.
* Review the sample question, understanding exactly how the test works and which elements of your verbal reasoning skills are being assessed.
* Avoid over-confidence and casualness. Skim reading any part of the test, including the instructions, is a mistake as it increases the likelihood that you will overlook significant details or make mistakes that are easily avoidable.

* Remember that if you are unsure or get stuck on a question, move on to the next one – you can always return to unfinished questions at the end if time allows.
* Highlight 'command' words in the test instructions – those words telling you what you have to do.
* Check frequently to ensure you are answering each question in the correct space provided.
* Guessing is to be avoided, but if you are uncertain about an answer to a question, go for your best reasoned choice.
* Keep focused and concentrate as much as you can throughout the test. You have a great deal of ground to cover, so don't let up until the work is complete.
* Do not allow your mind to become distracted. Focus solely on answering each question correctly and completing the test in the time allowed.
* Leave a few minutes at the end to check your test answers.

Above all, be positive and remain confident – the fact that you are reading this is a testament to your dedication and desire to succeed, and that will take you a long way to achieving your goal. Stay focused, positive and confident.

Test papers

It is helpful to obtain specimen papers. If you do not have access to past papers, find out what will be expected of you by contacting whoever is responsible for administering them. One of the main reasons for looking at past papers is that our minds work best when they are dealing with familiar processes. We feel more relaxed and in control of the situation. Shocks when you are sitting down with the test paper in front of you will waste your energy and interfere with your ability to concentrate. Moreover, it is helpful to tackle tests under timed conditions, as this gives you a good idea of what to expect, allows you to increase your speed and highlights any difficulties that require attention. Familiarity is extremely useful in creating the right conditions for you to work well under pressure.

Assistance

If possible, it is useful to discuss the tests with another person you trust, especially if they have already sat similar tests. Having this support helps you not only to maintain your commitment and sense of purpose but also to improve your results.

Improving your English skills

The first piece of advice professional writers will give to the question 'how do I improve my communication skills?' is read more and read a variety of writing styles used for different purposes. By reading more, you will see how language works and how it is used, which will enrich your own style. When you read, learn to be critical and analytical. It is surprising how often opinion masquerades as fact. Being a critical reader will improve your mental powers and skill, while boosting your confidence. When reading, do not ignore words that you do not understand simply because you can get the gist of what is being communicated – always look them up in a dictionary. Also, being attentive to what is being said or written will improve your own listening and presentational skills.

On the day

You must plan to arrive at the test centre in a state that is conducive to achieving your best possible score. This means being calm and focused. It is possible that you may feel nervous before the test, but you can help yourself by preparing in advance the practical details that will enable you to do well. Remember, it is unlikely that you are the only person who is feeling nervous; what is important is how you deal with your nerves! The following suggestions may help you to overcome unnecessary test-related anxiety.

1 Know where the test centre is located, and estimate how long it will take you to get there – plan your 'setting off time'. Now plan to leave 45 minutes before your setting off time to allow for travel delays. This way, you can be

more or less certain that you will arrive at the test centre in good time. If, for any reason, you think you will miss the start of the session, call the administrator to ask for instructions.

2   Try to get a good night's sleep before the test. This is obvious advice and, realistically, it is not always possible, particularly if you are prone to nerves the night before a test. However, you can take some positive steps to help. Consider taking a hot bath before you go to bed, drinking herbal rather than caffeinated tea, and doing some exercise.

3   The night before the test, organize everything that you need to take with you. This includes test instructions, directions, your identification, pens, erasers, possibly your calculator (with new batteries in it), reading glasses and contact lenses.

4   Decide what you are going to wear and have your clothes ready the night before. Be prepared for the test centre to be unusually hot or cold, and dress in layers so that you can regulate the climate yourself. If your test will be preceded or followed by an interview, make sure you dress accordingly for the interview, which is likely to be a more formal event than the test itself.

5   Eat breakfast! Even if you usually skip breakfast, you should consider that insufficient sugar levels affect you concentration and that a healthy breakfast might help you to concentrate, especially towards the end of the test when you are likely to be tired.

6   If you know that you have specific or exceptional requirements which will require preparation on the day, be sure to inform the test administrators in advance so that they can assist you as necessary. This may include wheelchair access, the availability

of the test in Braille or a facility for those with hearing difficulties. Similarly, if you are feeling unusually unwell on the day of the test, make sure that the test administrator is aware of it.

7   If, when you read the test instructions, there is something you don't understand, ask for clarification from the administrator. The time given to you to read the instructions may or may not be limited but, within the allowed time, you can usually ask questions. Don't assume that you have understood the instructions if, at first glance, they appear to be similar to the instructions for the practice tests.

8   Don't read through all the questions before you start. This simply wastes time. Start with Question 1 and work swiftly and methodically through each question in order. Unless you are taking a computerized test, where the level of difficulty of the next question depends on you correctly answering the previous question (such as the GMAT or GRE), don't waste time on questions that you know require a lot of time. You can return to these questions at the end if you have time left over.

9   After you have taken the test, find out the mechanism for feedback, and approximately the number of days you will have to wait to find out your results. Ask whether there is scope for objective feedback on your performance for your future reference.

10   Celebrate that you have finished.

Further sources of practice

In this final section you will find a list of useful sources for all types of psychometric tests.

Books

Bolles, Richard N., *What Color Is Your Parachute?* Berkeley, CA: Ten Speed Press, 2007.

Carter, P. and K. Russell, *Psychometric Testing: 1000 Ways to Assess Your Personality, Creativity, Intelligence and Lateral Thinking*. Chichester: John Wiley, 2001.

Jackson, Tom, *The Perfect Résumé*. New York: Broadway Books, 2004.

Krannich, Ronald L. and Caryl Rae Krannich, *Network Your Way to Job and Career Success*. Manassa, VA: Impact Publications, 1989.

Nuga, Simbo, *Succeed at Psychometric Testing: Practice Tests for Verbal Reasoning Intermediate*. London: Hodder Education, 2008.

Rhodes, Peter, *Succeed at Psychometric Testing: Practice Tests for Critical Verbal Reasoning*. London: Hodder Education, 2008.

Rhodes, Peter, *Succeed at Psychometric Testing: Practice Tests for Diagrammatic and Abstract Reasoning*. London: Hodder Education, 2008.

Vanson, Sally, *Succeed at Psychometric Testing: Practice Tests for Data Interpretation*. London: Hodder Education, 2008.

Walmsley, Bernice, *Succeed at Psychometric Testing: Practice Tests for Numerical Reasoning Advanced*. London: Hodder Education, 2008.

Walmsley, Bernice, *Succeed at Psychometric Testing: Practice Tests for Numerical Reasoning Intermediate*. London: Hodder Education, 2008.

Walmsley, Bernice, *Succeed at Psychometric Testing: Practice Tests for the National Police Selection Process*. London: Hodder Education, 2008.

Test publishers and suppliers

ASE
Chiswick Centre
414 Chiswick High Road

London W4 5TF
telephone: 0208 996 3337
www.ase-solutions.co.uk

Oxford Psychologists Press
Elsfield Hall
15–17 Elsfield Way
Oxford OX2 8EP
telephone: 01865 404500
www.opp.co.uk

Psytech International Ltd
The Grange
Church Road
Pulloxhill
Bedfordshire MK45 5HE
telephone: 01525 720003
www.psytech.co.uk

Verbal reasoning advanced level

SHL
The Pavilion
1 Atwell Place
Thames Ditton
Surrey KT7 0SR
telephone: 0208 398 4170
www.shl.com

The Psychological Corporation
Harcourt Assessment
Halley Court
Jordan Hill
Oxford OX2 8EJ
www.tpc-international.com

The Test Agency Ltd
Burgner House

4630 Kingsgate
Oxford Business Park South
Oxford OX4 2SU
telephone: 01865 402900
www.testagency.com

Other useful websites

Websites are liable to change, but the following are correct at the time of going to press.

www.careerpsychologycentre.com
www.deloitte.co.uk/index.asp
www.ets.org
www.mensa.org.uk
www.morrisby.co.uk
www.newmonday.co.uk
www.oneclickhr.com
www.pgcareers.com/apply/how/recruitment.asp
www.psychtesting.org.uk
www.psychtests.com
www.publicjobs.gov.ie
www.puzz.com
www.tests-direct.com

Other useful organizations

Association of Recognised English Language Schools (ARELS) – www.englishuk.com

Australian Psychological Society – www.psychology.org.au

The Best Practice Club – www.bpclub.com

The British Psychological Society – www.bps.org.uk

Canadian Psychological Association – www.cpa.ca

The Chartered Institute of Marketing – www.cim.co.uk

The Chartered Institute of Personnel and Development – www.cipd.co.uk

The Chartered Management Institute – www.managers.org.uk

Psyconsult – www.psyconsult.co.uk

Singapore Psychological Society –
www.singaporepsychologicalsociety.org

Society for Industrial and Organisational Assessment
(South Africa) (SIOPSA) – www.siopsa.org.za